Contents

page

Sounds in this book

a (grass)   all (tallest)   ay (away)   ea (leaps)
ey (monkey)   ind (find)   old (cold)
ou (you, out)   ow (snow, howler)
ph (elephant)   ue (blue)   wh (whale)

Let's go on safari!

On safari, you can visit Africa, the Arctic, the Amazon rainforest and Australia.

What animals will you see? What can you find out about them?

Amazon rainforest

Arctic

Africa

Australia

Africa

Lots of interesting animals are found in the grasslands of Africa.

This animal's feet are as big as plates!

This is the tallest animal of all.
It can run as fast as a car.

ho

long neck

The elephant is the biggest land animal.

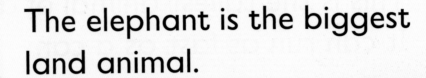 know **?**

Elephants can cry.

tusk to dig

trunk to put food into the elephant's mouth

ears to help the
elephant cool down

This family group of lions is called a pride.

Only a male lion has a mane.

A baby lion is called a cub.

Did you know ?

You can hear a
lion's roar from
five miles away.

A female lion is
called a lioness.

9

The Arctic

In cold snowy places, like the Arctic, some animals have white fur.
This helps them blend in with the snow all around them.

This animal's thick fur keeps out the cold.

The Arctic fox has lots of fur on its feet.

Some Arctic animals have big feet to run fast on the snow.

You can see this kind of whale in cold seas. These whales swim in groups called pods and make a noise like a whistle.

Did you know ?

These whales eat fish.

tail

mouth

flippers

13

Amazon rainforest

These monkeys are found in hot, wet rainforests.

The spider monkey uses its tail to swing from tree to tree.

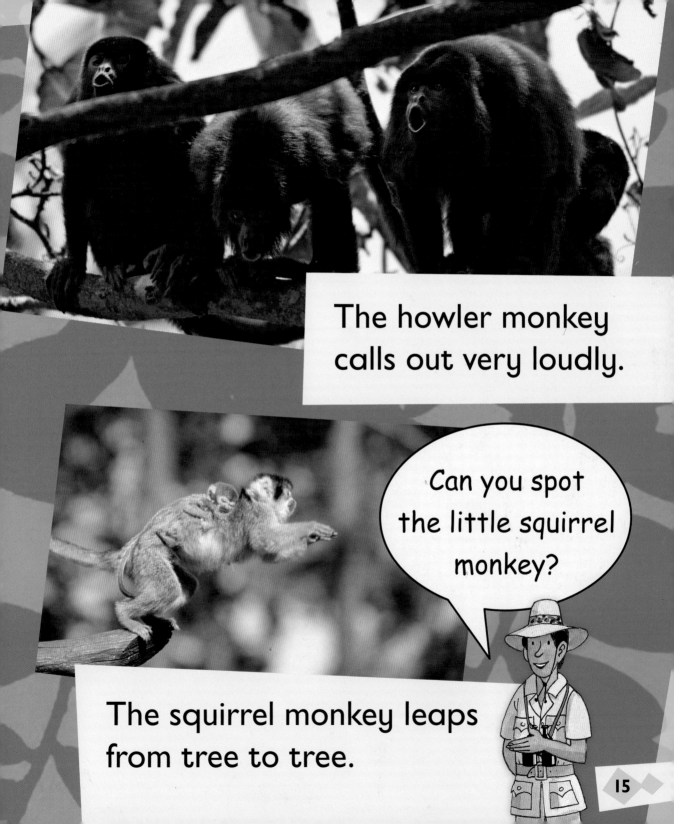

The howler monkey calls out very loudly.

Can you spot the little squirrel monkey?

The squirrel monkey leaps from tree to tree.

Look at these fantastic rainforest animals.

Tomato frog

red body

Toucan

The toucan uses its bill to crack nuts and seeds.

Blue Morpho butterfly

The biggest Blue Morpho butterflies are 20cm wide!

Australia

If you go on safari in Australia you may see a kangaroo.

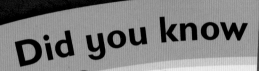
Did you know ?

A joey stays inside its mum's pouch.

A kangaroo hops on its back legs.
It can jump very high.
A baby kangaroo is called a joey.

joey

pouch

This animal is found in Australia too.

It likes to sit and eat in gum trees. It sleeps in the day and wakes up at night.

Quiz

What did you find out on your safari?

What is a baby lion called?

What is an elephant's trunk for?

Why do some Arctic animals have big feet?

What can a spider monkey use its tail for?

How do kangaroos get around?

Index